Religions of the World

Hinduism

Rasamandala Das

WORLD ALMANAC® LIBRARY

Please visit our web site at: www.worldalmanaclibrary.com
For a free color catalog describing World Almanac® Library's list of high-quality
books and multimedia programs, call 1-800-848-2928 (USA) or 1-800-387-3178
(Canada). World Almanac® Library's fax: (414) 332-3567.

Library of Congress Cataloging-in-Publication Data

Das, Rasamandala.
     Hinduism / by Rasamandala Das.
         p. cm. — (Religions of the world)
     Includes bibliographical references and index.
     ISBN 0-8368-5867-0 (lib. bdg.)
     ISBN 0-8368-5873-5 (softcover)
     1. Hinduism—Juvenile literature. I. Title.
     II. Religions of the world (Milwaukee, Wis.)
     BL1203.D37   2005
     294.5—dc22   2005041749

This edition first published in 2006 by
World Almanac® Library
330 West Olive Street, Suite 100
Milwaukee, WI 53212 USA

This edition copyright © 2006 by World Almanac® Library. Original edition copyright © 2005 by
Hodder Wayland. First published in 2005 by Hodder Wayland, an imprint of Hodder Children's Books,
a division of Hodder Headline Limited, 338 Euston Road, London NW1 3BH, U.K.

Subject consultant: Dr. Nick Sutton, The Oxford Centre for Hindu Studies
Project Editor, Hodder Wayland: Kirsty Hamilton
Editor: Nicola Barber
Designer: Janet McCallum
Picture Researcher: Shelley Noronha, Glass Onion Pictures
Maps and artwork: Peter Bull
World Almanac® Library editor: Gini Holland
World Almanac® Library cover design: Kami Koenig

Photo Credits
The publisher would like to thank the following for permission to reproduce their pictures:
Alamy/Saulius T. Kondrotas 10; The Bhaktivedanta Book Trust International. Copyright 2005. Used with
permission 13; Bhaktivedanta Manor 45; © Biju Boro/AFP/Getty Images: cover; CIRCA Photo Library/Bipin J.
Mistry 4, John Smith 18, Bipin J. Mistry 23, Bipin J. Mistry 24, John Smith 27, Bipin J. Mistry 29;
Corbis/Lindsay Hebberd 32; Eye Ubiquitous 41; Friends of Vrindavan 44; Robert Harding Picture Library A.
Tovy 11, A. Tovy 14, J.H.C. Wilson 22, J. Sweeney 30, A. Tovy 34, S. Grandadam 36; Hare Krishna Food for
Life 42; Impact Photos 40; ISKCON Educational Services 21, 43; Ann and Bury Peerless 7, 9, 16, 17, 20, 25,
33; Photofusion 39; Rex Pictures Ltd/Jeremy Hunter 31; Topfoto 15, 19, 35, 38; ZUL 28

Printed in China

1 2 3 4 5 6 7 8 9 09 08 07 06 05

Contents

Note

In the Western world, years are numbered as either B.C. ("Before Christ") or A.D. (Anno Domini, which is Latin for "In the year of our Lord"). In this series, the more neutral terms B.C.E. ("Before the Common Era") and C.E. ("Common Era") are used.

Introduction

Hinduism is perhaps the oldest surviving religion in the world. It is difficult to say with certainty how it started. Unlike most other religions, it has no single founder, no one scripture, and no commonly agreed upon set of teachings. Throughout its long history, many important religious leaders have taught different philosophies and written many holy books. For this reason, scholars often refer to Hinduism as "a family of religions" or "a way of life."

Sanatan Dharma

Hinduism is at least four thousand years old. Many Hindus prefer to call their tradition *Sanatan Dharma*, meaning "the eternal religion." This name suggests a religion that is timeless, teaching truths (such as the existence of the eternal soul) relevant to all people at all times. Consequently, most Hindus do not reject other religions, believing them to be different paths toward the common goal of linking the soul with God. Hinduism is certainly closely connected with other Eastern traditions such as Jainism, Sikhism, and Buddhism.

The Vedas

It is hard for everyone to agree on what is meant by Hinduism. Many Hindus say it refers to practices based on the teachings of certain holy books. These are the *Vedas* and their supplements (books based on the *Vedas*). *Veda* is a Sanskrit word meaning "knowledge." This ancient wisdom was first passed down orally and only later written down (*see page 7*). Many scholars believe that the first book, the *Rig Veda*, was compiled between 1500 and 1000 B.C.E. but was written down about 400 B.C.E. The *Vedas* themselves do not mention the modern terms *Hindu* and *Hinduism*. They talk about *dharma*, which roughly translates as "religious law" or "religious duty" (*see page 14*).

AUM BHURBHUVAHSWAH:
TATSAVITURVARENYAM
BHARGODEVASYADHIMAHI:
DHIYOYONAHPRACHODAYAT

▲ The written Sanskrit sign for Om *is often used as the symbol of Hinduism.* Om *is believed to represent the sound of creation. Hinduism teaches about the idea of successive creations, believing there is no absolute beginning or end to time. For this reason, Hindus often prefer to call their tradition* Sanatan Dharma *(the eternal religion).*

▶ *This map shows where Hindus live in the world today and some places in India mentioned in the text.*

The Hindu Tradition

It is clear that what we now call "Hinduism" has its roots in ancient India. Some scholars say the religion was brought into India by a group of people, known as Aryans, who invaded from Central Asia in about 1500 B.C.E. Many Hindus dispute this, claiming that the Hindu tradition grew up in India itself, well before this time. The Hindu tradition often differs with Western ideas of time and evolution, claiming that human history (and its own heritage) go back indefinitely to previous glorious ages (*see page 6*).

Although Hinduism is complicated, there are three main strands:

1. *Vaishnavas*—who worship Vishnu (or his forms such as Rama and Krishna)

2. *Shaivas*—who worship Shiva (*see page 15*)

3. *Shaktas*—who worship Shakti, the goddess, usually in her form as Shiva's wife (*see page 16*)

In practice, many Hindus don't officially follow any of these strands—nor do they restrict themselves to just one. They often worship a number of deities. For this reason, and its general acceptance of other religions, Hinduism is known for being inclusive and tolerant. It is also misunderstood as being polytheistic (believing in many gods); in fact, most Hindus believe in one Supreme God.

Hinduism Worldwide

Although Hinduism is connected to India, its traditions and practices have now spread throughout the world. Major migration began in the nineteenth century, when Hindus went to live in places such as Fiji, Mauritius, the Caribbean, and South and East Africa. Many more moved in the late 1960s and early 1970s. There are now large communities of Hindus worldwide, especially in Europe and North America. India itself has many religions, but today more than 80 percent of its people follow the Hindu tradition.

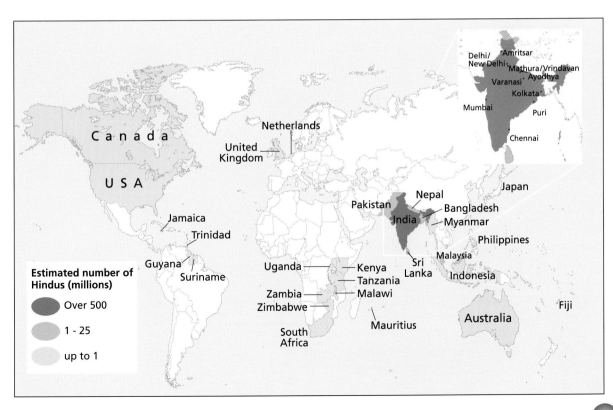

History and Development of Hinduism

For a number of reasons, Hinduism's early history is complex and the subject of many theories. First of all, major differences of opinion exist between Hindus and Western researchers. Also, Hinduism is not a single religion, but includes many different branches. In addition, Hinduism has no definite starting point. It goes back at least four thousand years, and maybe much further. To study Hinduism thoroughly, it is important to understand its own world view and its understanding of time itself.

The Roots of the Tradition

Hindus believe that time is eternal and that it moves in cycles of four ages (*yugas*), much like the four seasons. Apparently, during the first age—called the golden age—people were kind and religious. We now live in the fourth age—the iron age—typified by cruelty and materialism. Hindu people therefore question the idea that humans are always progressing. They also believe that genuine religion is eternal (Sanatan Dharma) and universal. It is not limited to one time, one country, or any particular group of people.

Many scholars believe that Hinduism originated largely outside India. The Aryan invasion theory suggests that the Aryans conquered the Indus valley (in present-day Pakistan) about 1500 B.C.E. The Aryans worshiped many deities connected with nature, especially Indra, the god of rain. They also brought with them the Sanskrit language, which has links to many European languages. Sanskrit is the origin of Hindi, the dominant Indian language today, and remains the language of Hindu prayer and study. The Aryans may also have brought their own social system with its different classes or *varnas* (*see pages 14 and 37*). Their own

beliefs and practices may have mixed with those of the local Indus peoples, giving rise to what we now call Hinduism.

▼ *This diagram shows how the wheel of time rolls along in endless cycles of four ages. Hindus say we are now just after the start of the fourth, shortest age, the age of iron. After this, the next golden age begins.*

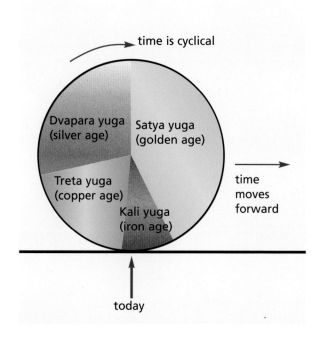

time is cyclical

Dvapara yuga (silver age)

Satya yuga (golden age)

Treta yuga (copper age)

Kali yuga (iron age)

time moves forward

today

The Books Are Written

The teachings of Hinduism, initially passed down orally, were later written down. Tradition states that a sage called Vyasa recorded them on palm leaves about five thousand years ago, at the beginning of this age, the *Kali* yuga. Scholars such as Shankara and Ramanuja say that the first books, the *Vedas*, were composed later, from about 1000 B.C.E. onward. During this period, the most common religious practice was the sacred fire ceremony, performed in honor of nature deities such as Indra, god of rain, and Agni, god of fire.

Later, the *Puranas* were composed, containing many of the stories still popular today. Scholars believe that most were written down between 500 B.C.E. and 500 C.E. During this period, the fire ceremony was superceded by *puja*—the ritual worship of sacred images. Indra and Agni were no longer the main deities, but were largely replaced by Vishnu, Shiva, and Shakti (also called Devi, the goddess). Two religions related to Hinduism, Buddhism and Jainism, also flourished during this time.

Poets and Theologians

From about 500 C.E. onward, important thinkers laid the foundations for modern Hinduism. In the south of India, saints wrote hundreds of devotional poems, still recited in temples today. Among these saints was a woman called Andal, who continues to be venerated in southern India.

Later, beginning about 800 C.E., scholars wrote detailed explanations of the sacred texts. They also developed their own specific doctrines, each passed down by an unbroken chain of *gurus* (teachers) and their disciples, known as a *sampradaya*. During this period, these thinkers developed two main ideas:

1. God is everywhere (and is everything).

2. God is also a person (separate from the world).

▼ *Excavations at the ancient Indus valley city of Mohenjo-daro, now in modern Pakistan. Scholars say that archaeological and other evidence from such sites suggests that northwest India was invaded by the Aryans, who brought with them the beginnings of Hinduism.*

The Mogul Period

From the eighth century onward, the new religion of Islam reached India via traders plying the Arabian Sea and by the Muslim armies that conquered the northwest province of Sind. Muslim political power in India began with the Turks about 1200 C.E. and culminated in the Mogul Empire, which ruled India from 1526. The most famous Mogul emperor, Akbar (1542–1605), was extremely liberal and broad-minded and allowed Hindus to practice their faith freely. His great grandson, Aurangzeb, however, was ruthless, destroying temples and restricting Hindus in their practices. During the Mogul period, Hindus were somewhat excluded from public life.

The British Period

A British victory at the Battle of Plassey in 1757 heralded the end of the Mogul Empire and the rise of British supremacy in India. At first, the British did not interfere with the religion and culture of the Indian people, allowing Hindus to practice their religion with little outside influence. Later, however, missionaries arrived, determined to bring Christianity and their own versions of civilization to India.

The Reform Movements

In response, a number of Hindu reform movements arose. Hindu thinkers became influenced by Western thought, and while some adopted Western philosophical ideas and aspects of Christianity, others opposed them. In 1828, Rama Mohan Roy established the Brahmo Sabha, incorporating ideas from both Christianity and from seventeenth and eighteenth-century philosophers such as John Locke and David Hume. Other groups, such as the Arya Samaj, objected to attempts to convert Indians to Christianity. They tried to protect Hinduism while freeing it from what they saw as its superstitious aspects, such as the worship of the *murti* (sacred image).

One of the most successful movements, establishing centers worldwide, was the Ramakrishna mission. It was founded in 1897 by the monk Vivekananda, who named it after his own spiritual teacher, Ramakrishna. Vivekananda impressed the Western world with his presentation on Hinduism to the World Parliament of Religions at Chicago in 1893. He won a standing ovation by addressing the audience as "Sisters and Brothers of America." He subsequently presented a vision of religion that was inclusive and universal, based on the Hindu idea of the soul within all species of life.

The Bhakti Saints

The restraints of the Mogul era were made worse for many people by the tight control kept by Hindu priests. Many of these brahmins, *members of the highest class, insisted on compliance with the hereditary caste system, which did not permit Hindus of lower birth to take significant roles in society or to advance in spiritual life. As a result, ordinary Hindus felt oppressed, and leaders rose from among the people. These saints, known as the* bhakti *saints, emphasized the spiritual equality of everyone and the need for personal morality and a mood of service. They expressed their religious feelings through song, music, and poetry. A wave of devotion (bhakti) swept across India between 1400 and 1700.*

A Poem by Mirabai

*"We do not get a human life
Simply by asking.
Birth as a human
Is the reward for good deeds
In former births.
Life waxes and wanes imperceptibly,
And stays not long.
The leaf that has fallen
Returns not to the branch.
Behold the Sea of Reincarnation
With its swift, irresistible tide!
O Krishna, O pilot of my soul,
Swiftly conduct my ship to the
  other shore.
Mira, the servant of Krishna, declares,
'Life lasts for but a few days only.'"*

Mirabai was one of the main bhakti saints, and her poems are still popular today. They speak of her tireless devotion to Lord Krishna, one of the main Hindu deities. They also refer to other important Hindu ideas, such as karma, reincarnation, and moksha, *or liberation (see page 13).*

◄ *Swami Vivekananda. His teachings grew out of the growing contact between India and the West. Other reformers promoted a different type of Hinduism, connected with nationalism and a strong sense of Indian identity. Most important of these latter was Mahatma Gandhi (see page 38) who opposed British domination of India and the depletion of the country's immense wealth. He was instrumental in India's gaining independence.*

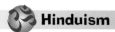
Independent India

The partition (division) of India in 1947 into two separate countries—Pakistan and India—was accompanied by considerable violence. Large numbers of Muslims headed for the newly created and predominantly Muslim Pakistan. Many Hindus and Sikhs fled in the opposite direction, seeking refuge within the newly drawn boundaries of India. Bloody clashes occurred between the two streams of refugees—between communities that had previously lived together in relative harmony. These upheavals reinforced the emerging ideas of India being a Hindu country and of Hinduism being an Indian religion.

Hinduism Goes Global

In the 1960s, many Hindus began to migrate to the West, especially to Britain and the United States. At the same time, many Hindu gurus (religious teachers) traveled to the West. They helped support the growing Hindu communities and started missionary movements that attracted Western interest. Many Westerners began to practice meditation and *hatha yoga*, a form of exercise that nurtures inner peace (*see page 25*).

In the late 1960s, the Transcendental Meditation organization became popular throughout the world, and its spiritual leader, Maharishi Mahesh Yogi, attracted the attention of celebrities such as the Beatles. One of the most conspicuous groups at the time was the Hare Krishna movement, whose male followers shaved their heads and wore traditional saffron-colored robes.

▼ *Members of the Hare Krishna Movement in the U.S. Although termed a "new religious movement," the organization goes back to Chaitanya, one of the bhakti saints. Its members became famous worldwide for their chanting and dancing in the streets of towns and cities.*

Modern Hinduism

During the late part of the twentieth century, Hindu groups and communities became well-established throughout the developed world. Far and wide, in North America, Britain, South Africa, and Australia, Hindu people flourished socially, academically, and economically. At the hearts of their communities, they built expensive and impressive new temples.

In India itself, religious unrest continued. In 1984, tensions between the Hindu and Sikh communities came to a head when government forces stormed the Sikh headquarters, the Golden Temple in Amritsar. The subsequent assassination of Prime Minister Indira Gandhi, apparently by her Sikh bodyguards, further strained relationships between the previously close communities. Violence between Hindus and Muslims continued too, for example in the late 1990s, when there were angry clashes over the Islamic mosque built at Ayodhya, the birthplace of Rama, an important Hindu deity (*see page 19*). There was also continuing controversy over apparent attempts to convert Hindus to other religions, such as Christianity and Buddhism.

These historical trends have prompted modern Hindus to try to redefine their tradition, often as a separate religion. Despite these changes, the ancient tradition continues to flourish, primarily as a path toward spiritual and social well-being. Hinduism now extends well beyond India, nurtured by a number of well-organized movements with followers throughout the world.

▼ *The Swami Narayana Temple in London was opened in 1995. It is built of marble in a traditional Indian style of architecture. The Swami Narayana Mission has temples worldwide and is headed by a well-known guru, Pramukh Swami.*

Hindu Teachings and Holy Books

Hindus do not place much importance on everyone believing the same thing. They stress more the need for sincere spiritual practice and the courage for humans to sometimes change their minds. Despite this flexible approach toward belief, some ideas are shared by practically all Hindus. These include the atman (soul), reincarnation, karma, and moksha (liberation). Although belief in God is widely accepted, opinions differ among Hindus about God's nature and identity.

Atman—The Eternal Soul

Hindus believe that the atman is the "real self" or the "soul." It is eternal and made of *brahman* (spirit). The mind and the body are made of matter.

In the religious text the *Bhagavad Gita* (*see page 20*), Krishna (one of the forms of Vishnu) explained how, for all of us, the body is changing at every moment. At the same time, we (the atman, the real self within the body) remain the same throughout our lives, despite changes to the mind and body. Krishna compared the body to a vehicle and the soul to the driver. He also compared the body to clothes, which eventually wear out, and therefore finally need replacing.

Reincarnation

Hindus believe that the atman, or soul, leaves the body at the time of death. It is carried in the astral body, which includes the mind, to a new body. This new body could be another human body, or the soul may be elevated to the higher, heavenly planets. A third option is that it enters the lower species, to be born again as a plant, fish, insect, bird, or beast.

Hindus believe that awareness, and therefore the atman, is present in all species of life. This idea forms the basis for certain values (such as *ahimsa*, nonviolence) and practices (such as vegetarianism).

The Law of Karma

Hindus believe that our next birth depends on our karma. Karma literally means "action," but it also means "the results of one's

Spirit and Matter

Spirit (brahman)	Matter
Never-changing	*Ever-changing*
Eternal	*Temporary*
Conscious	*Unconscious*
Dynamic	*Inert*

"*Those who are seers of the truth have concluded that matter (the body) is always changing and that spirit (the real self) never changes. This they have concluded by studying the nature of both.*"

(Bhagavad Gita 2.16)

actions." Hindus therefore say kind and charitable actions bringing "good karma," and cruel acts bring "bad karma." Each soul is responsible for its actions.

In Hindu belief, the soul only creates karma while in the human body. Animals have no moral choice—they act purely according to their instincts. They must wait to come into the human form again before making free choices. Those souls who go to the heavenly worlds enjoy themselves but return to earth as humans after using up their good karma.

Moksha

The cycle of birth and death is called *samsara*. Hindus believe it goes on indefinitely but is not eternal. While in human form, the soul can come to understand his or her true nature as brahman (spirit). To do this, he or she must become free from all karma and all selfish desires. The soul can then attain moksha, liberation from the cycle of repeated birth and death. Moksha is a state of *yoga*, which means "union with God." Yoga also refers to any process of linking with the divine.

▼ *This modern painting symbolically depicts* samsara, *the perpetual cycle of birth and death. It is based on a verse from the* Bhagavad Gita, *which states, "As the soul passes within the body from childhood to youth to old age, similarly at death the unchanging self passes into a new body."*

Dharma

Dharma is often translated as "religion" or "religious duty." Dharma actually means "duties that sustain us according to who we are." The idea is that one has different duties according to one's identity. There are two types of dharma:

1. Sanatan Dharma—the eternal relationship between the soul and God

2. Varnashrama Dharma—duties according to the body one has, involving the four varnas (classes) and the four *ashramas* (stages of life)

The system of four varnas has become what is referred to as the "caste system" (*see page 37 for more about the caste system*). The four ashramas are the four stages of life (*see box, page 38*).

▲ *A sadhu (holy man). This man has dedicated his life to serving God. For Hindus, there are four aims to human life: to become moral and righteous, to create prosperity, to enjoy worldly pleasure in an ethical way, and to get liberation from the perpetual cycle of birth and death. The last aim is most important, the final goal.*

One Goal, Many Paths

The final goal of all dharma is moksha, liberation. Although there is only one goal, there are many different ways to achieve it. There are four main paths, or yogas:

1. *Karma-yoga*—the path of selfless work

2. *Jnana-yoga*—the path of knowledge and wisdom

3. *Astanga-yoga*—the path of meditation

4. *Bhakti-yoga*—the path of devotional service

Many Hindus strive to follow one or more of these paths. Most believe that members of other religious traditions also follow these paths in their own ways.

Four Varnas

Shudra—craftsperson, worker
Vaishya—farmer, trader, business
Kshatriya—police, army, government
Brahmin—priest, teacher, intellectual

Four Ashramas

Brahmachari Ashrama—student life
Grihastha Ashrama—householder life
Vanaprashta Ashrama—retired life
Sannyasa Ashrama—renounced life

God

Hindu people usually refer to God as "Bhagwan" or, less often, "Ishvara." The Hindu teachings say that God can be found in three places:

1. Everywhere, as brahman, the all-pervading spirit. God is aware of everything. The soul (atman) is a part of God and is also brahman (eternal and conscious).

2. Within the heart of all living beings. God can be detected in animals as instinct and in humans as conscience, inspiration, and exceptional ability.

3. Outside—far beyond this world. God lives in the eternal, spiritual world.

The Trimurti

Although God is one, he has unlimited forms and qualities. These are represented by the thousands of Hindu deities. There are three main deities, called the *trimurti*. Brahma is the creator, Vishnu the maintainer, and Shiva the destroyer. All matter goes through three phases that correspond to these deities: creation, staying for some time, and final destruction. Some Hindus say that these deities are all equal. Others claim that one is Supreme (usually Vishnu or Shiva), while the others are subordinate and less powerful.

➤ *Shiva the destroyer. His followers, called Shaivas, usually consider Shiva to be Supreme, and they make up one of the three main denominations, or "strands," within Hinduism* (see page 5). *In this painting, you can also see Brahma and Vishnu in the top left-hand corner. At the bottom left stands Shiva's wife, Shakti, or Parvati, with her and Shiva's son Ganesh, with his elephant head.*

Goddesses

Most Hindus believe God manifests in many forms and is both male and female. The three main deities, the trimurti, each has a wife. Sarasvati, the goddess of learning and the arts, is the wife of Brahma. Lakshmi, goddess of wealth and fortune, has Vishnu as her husband. Shakti, Mother Nature, has many different forms including Parvati, Durga, and Kali. She is Shiva's wife.

Worshipers of Shakti (also called Devi) make up the third main group within Hinduism (*see page 5*), known as Shaktas. They mainly worship Shakti as she appears in the form of Parvati or Durga (*see page 15*). Many Shaktas worship other goddesses, including Sarasvati and Lakshmi, who are considered to be Shakti's daughters.

In Our Own Words

"I am proud of my tradition for two reasons. First, it encourages a close personal relationship with God. Secondly, it is respectful to other religions. It doesn't say, 'You have to follow this particular religion.' After all, there is one God for all of us!"

▼ *Goddess Sarasvati is shown here with her husband Brahma, the creator, who has four heads. Sarasvati is said to have cursed her husband and, as a result, although he is honored by most Hindus, he is worshiped in only one place—a town called Pushkar in India.*

Forms and Avatars of God

In addition to the trimurti and their wives, there are many other deities, including:

- Rama and Krishna, two important *avatars* ("descents," or "incarnations") of Vishnu.

- Hanuman, the monkey-warrior. He is physically powerful and, as Rama's devoted servant, helped Rama rescue Sita (*see page 19*). Hanuman is a favorite with sportspeople and soldiers and is worshiped for help and good fortune.

- Ganesh and Skanda, sons of Shiva and Shakti. Ganesh is famous for his elephant's head and, as the remover of obstacles, is venerated before any important event. His brother, Skanda, is popular in southern India, where he is known as Murugan.

- Surya, the sun god, is often considered a form of Vishnu. Surya is especially worshiped during the festival of Pongal in southern India. Many other gods have responsibility for running

the universe; these include Chandra (the moon god), Agni (in charge of fire), Vayu (the wind god), Yama (the god of death and justice) and Indra (the god of rain and king of the heavens). These deities, popular in early Hinduism, are rarely worshiped individually these days.

➤ *Vishnu, the sustainer, with his wife Lakshmi, goddess of wealth and good fortune. Vishnu's followers are called Vaishnavas, one of the three largest Hindu denominations. They usually think of Vishnu as God, the Supreme Deity. Vishnu is famous for his avatars ("descents," or "incarnations"), the most popular of which are Rama and Krishna (see page 19).*

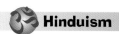

The Religious Texts

Hindus largely base their ideas on religious texts. The two main groups of texts are called *shruti* and *smriti*. The shruti texts are considered by many Hindus to be more important, but they are philosophical and hard to understand. The smriti help to explain the shruti, often through stories.

The Four Vedas

The first texts were called the *Vedas*. There are four main books including the oldest, the *Rig Veda* (see page 4). An important part of the *Vedas* are the philosophical texts called the *Upanishads*. The *Upanishads* are one of four broad categories within the *Vedas*. Although they may be interspersed within the *Vedas*, they have also been compiled as separate books.

The ideas in the *Vedas* and the *Upanishads* are further discussed in an important book called the V*edanta Sutra*, part of the smriti. *Vedanta* means the "conclusion of the *Vedas*." *Sutra* means an aphorism—a saying that is short but which has deep meanings contained within it.

Main Hindu Holy Books

Shruti ("that which is heard")
The Vedas *(prayers and philosophy)*
The Upanishads *(philosophy)*

Smriti ("that which is remembered")
The Vedanta Sutra *(aphorisms)*
The Puranas *(stories and histories)*
The epics: *(1)* The Ramayana
               (2) The Mahabharata
The Bhagavad Gita *(philosophy)*

The Puranas

The *Puranas* are books of ancient stories, or myths ("Purana" means "ancient"). Many Hindus do not consider myths to be untrue. Rather, they believe that myths describe other dimensions which are often beyond this world. Most of the *Puranas* are dedicated to Shiva (and Shakti) and to Vishnu, who appears in many forms and incarnations. Of the ten main incarnations of Vishnu, Rama and Krishna are the most important.

◄ *A gathering of people in India listen to a Hindu guru speak on a Hindu text.* Upanishad *means "sitting close to." It refers to the student who would sit near the guru, the spiritual teacher. In Hinduism, the guru is still considered important to help the student understand the* Vedas *and the other holy books.*

➤ *This thirteenth-century sculpture from Orissa in eastern India shows a scene from the* Devi Bhagavata Purana. *The story, in which Durga kills the buffalo demon, illustrates the powerful and assertive role that women play in both social and spiritual life in Hinduism.*

There are eighteen main *Puranas*. The most famous are those describing the activities of Krishna. Krishna is celebrated for his activities as a child and youth in the village of Vrindavana. As a baby, he was extremely mischievous, stealing butter and feeding it to the monkeys. As an adult, he moved to the city of Dvaraka and became a powerful king.

Another popular book, the *Devi Bhagavata Purana*, tells the story of the goddess Durga. She slayed a demon who took the form of a buffalo. All the gods combined could not kill the demon, but Durga easily defeated him.

The Ramayana

The *Ramayana* is one of two Hindu epics (the other being the *Mahabharata*). It means "the journey of Rama." It tells of how Lord Rama, an incarnation of Vishnu, was tricked into leaving his kingdom. His wife, Sita, and his brother, Lakshman, decided to go with him to the forest. While they were there, the wicked Ravana kidnapped Sita. In search of his dear wife, Rama met a race of powerful and intelligent monkeys and their general, the monkey-warrior, named Hanuman.

After long travels, Hanuman eventually found Sita, captive on the island of Lanka, Ravana's kingdom. With one huge leap, he returned to mainland India and assembled a monkey army on the southern coast. Under his direction, the troops constructed a floating bridge, marched onto Lanka, and defeated Ravana's forces. Rama killed Ravana and was reunited with his wife. In jubilation, the heroes returned home to Ayodhya. It was the night of the new moon and pitch dark. As the army entered the city, the citizens lit thousands of lamps to light up the way.

Verse from the Ramayana

"*If one surrenders unto me sincerely, saying 'My Lord, from this day on I am fully surrendered unto You,' from that time on I give that person protection. That is my vow.*"

—*Lord Rama to Hanuman*

The Mahabharata

The *Mahabharata* is the longest poem in the world. It recounts the story of the five Pandava brothers (the sons of King Pandu) and their one hundred cousins, headed by Duryodhana. The eldest of the Pandavas was the rightful heir to the throne of the Indian empire. In a game of dice, he was cheated out of his empire by Duryodhana. The Pandavas spent thirteen years in exile, but when they returned to claim their kingdom, Duryodhana refused to give it up. The Pandavas had no alternative but to fight. Armies from all over India assembled on the plains of Kurukshetra, just north of present-day New Delhi.

Lord Krishna had always supported the five Pandavas. Before the battle of Kurukshetra, Krishna offered the third brother, Arjuna, and his cousin, Duryodhana, a choice. Either they could have him (the Supreme Lord) on their side—but not in any fighting capacity—or they could employ the services of his army. Arjuna chose Krishna. Duryodhana scoffed at Arjuna's choice and chose Krishna's troops. Arjuna asked Krishna to be his charioteer. These events set the scene for Krishna to speak the *Bhagavad Gita*, which forms one chapter toward the end of the *Mahabharata*.

The Bhagavad Gita

As the armies made their final preparations, Arjuna asked Krishna to draw up his chariot between the two armies. He wanted to estimate the strength of the enemy. Seeing all his cousins, his grandfather, and his military teacher in the opposite ranks, he broke down and said, "Krishna, I shall not fight. I am confused about my duty. Please become my teacher and instruct me."

Krishna first praised Arjuna. As a warrior, he was not only brave but also considerate. He was concerned about how his actions would affect others. Then, however, Krishna criticized the prince for thinking that his body was his real self, and that his cousins were special because of some physical relationship. Krishna spoke the entire *Bhagavad Gita* to relieve Arjuna of this misconception, and to help him understand his true eternal, spiritual nature.

Arjuna and his brothers won the battle of Kurukshetra and took charge of the vast Indian Empire. After Lord Krishna left this world, some thirty-six years later, the five brothers retired to the Himalayas. Krishna's departure marked the beginning of Kali yuga, the age of hypocrisy and false leadership.

➤ *Krishna and Arjuna on the chariot just before the Battle of Kurukshetra. After hearing Krishna's instructions, Arjuna fought with determination, and after eighteen days he and his brothers emerged victorious. This Indian painting dates from the eighteenth century.*

3 Spiritual and Religious Practices

Many Hindus consider five practices essential to their spiritual well-being. These practices largely focus on developing awareness of their own spiritual nature and their relationship with the Supreme (God). The five basic practices are dharma, or living a virtuous life (see page 14), worship, festivals, pilgrimage, and rites of passage.

Worship

Hindu worship involves a wide range of practices—even dance is included! The most common practice is puja, ritual worship of the murti or sacred image. Puja is central to the process of bhakti-yoga, the path of devotion (*see page 14*).

▼ *A murti of Krishna wears flowers during temple puja.*

Types of Worship

- Yoga and meditation
- Havan—*the sacred fire ceremony*
- Pravachan—*a talk or lecture on the holy books* (see page 18)
- Puja—*ritual worship of the murti (sacred image).*

Puja may include other practices, such as:

- Darshan—*"seeing" the deity*
- Prasada—*offering and receiving sacred food* (see page 40)
- Arati—*a ceremony in which a lamp is offered* (see page 24)
- Seva—*active service to the murti*
- Bhajan and kirtan—*singing and chanting* (see page 10)
- Pradakshina—*circumambulation*

These practices are not solely in veneration of the murti. For example, arati may be offered to the guru or to other holy people; seva may be offered to the guru or spiritual community.

In Our Own Words

"On my altar at home I have a photo of my spiritual teacher. I offer arati to him each morning. The guru is not God, but because he is dear to God, we offer him respect and worship. We believe that we receive the grace of God by serving and pleasing those people who are dear to him."

▼ *People light lamps to perform the Akasa Deep puja, the "sky lantern" festival on the sacred River Ganges. Legend says that the Ganges water was touched by the sacred feet of Vishnu. Another tells a story of how Shiva caught the river in his hair as it fell to earth from heaven.*

Focuses of Worship

Although most Hindus believe in one God, there are many focuses of worship. For example, many Hindu deities (*see page 15*) are often worshiped through the murti.

Hindus also worship God as represented in other ways. They believe that anything connected to God is sacred. For this reason, they may venerate lesser deities (such as Surya, the sun god), spiritual teachers (gurus), and family elders, such as parents. They consider holy the land associated with a saint or incarnation of God, and many rivers are sacred (*see page 31*). Even the cow may be offered worship, because she represents the mother, and is therefore special. Some Hindus venerate holy trees, such as the tulsi (sacred basil) and the bilva. Hindus believe that without respecting what is dear to God, including all living beings, spiritual advancement is impossible.

Puja, or Ritual Worship

Hindus perform puja at home and in the temple. There is no special day of the week for puja, although different days are connected with specific deities, for example Shiva is often worshiped on a Monday. The time of day, however, is important. The tranquil morning hours, especially before dawn, are considered best for puja. Evening worship is also thought to be auspicious.

Worship is often a personal matter and can be performed alone, in prayer, and in meditation. Some traditions emphasize congregational practices, such as group singing. Worship in the temple is often quite informal, with visitors arriving and leaving throughout the public ceremonies.

Puja in the Temple

The temple is considered to be the home of God or of the particular deity represented on the shrine. These sacred images, or murtis, are served just like great kings or queens. The temple priests bathe them, dress them, and offer them food. Puja also involves offering auspicious items, such as pure water, perfume, and flower garlands. Worship usually finishes with the offering of vegetarian food to the murti.

Puja in the Home

Practically every Hindu home includes a shrine. It may simply be a shelf in the kitchen with framed pictures of deities and saints. Other families set aside an entire room, with a shrine housing small murtis. Worship in the home is usually a simplified version of the elaborate temple rituals. Women often take charge, and children learn about Hindu traditions by being actively involved.

▼ *Puja in the home in the United Kingdom (UK). It is usually the women of the household who take charge.*

In Our Own Words

"When I was small, I had my own shrine in the bedroom, with lots of pictures of Krishna, Rama, and everyone. Hanuman was my favorite. Now I often help Mom do the arati. All of our food is offered to God. My mom puts a little of each dish into stainless steel bowls on a tray. Then she puts the tray on the shrine and says some prayers while ringing a bell. Afterwards, we all say a prayer before eating."

Visiting the Temple

Although most Hindus worship daily at home, they also visit a temple regularly. Upon entering, they remove their shoes out of respect and for cleanliness. They come before the shrine to take darshan ("sight") of the deity. With palms together, they say a few prayers. It is customary to offer a gift of fruits, uncooked grains, or flowers, or to drop a few coins in the donation box. The priest may hand out morsels of *prasad*, sacred food offered to and blessed by the deity. Then the worshipers sit on the floor in the peaceful atmosphere and wait for the arati ceremony.

The Arati Ceremony

Many people gather for the arati. There are up to six or seven services during the day. In India, the first is usually before dawn, at about five or six o'clock. Standing in front of the shrine, the temple priest offers a lamp to the murtis. The lamp usually has five wicks. The lamp, now considered sacred, is passed around the worshipers. Each worshiper passes a palm over the flames, and then touches his or her fingers respectfully to the forehead. The priest also offers incense, water, and a flower.

During arati, it is customary for the congregation to stand. They may join in singing or chanting, with small hand cymbals, drums, and other musical instruments.

◄ *Hindu women wait for the arati ceremony at a temple in London, UK. In some temples, men sit on one side of the temple room, women on the other. There are usually no chairs, except for the elderly who have difficulty sitting on the floor.*

Yoga and Meditation

As well as being used for worship, the temple and home shrine are also places for quiet reflection and meditation. Hindu texts stress the importance of controlling the mind. It is risky to let it wander or to obey its every desire. Yoga and meditation are ways of disciplining the body and mind. Hatha yoga, with its postures and breathing exercises, is good for the physical health. Its main purpose, however, is to control and quiet the mind and then to see, directly, the soul and God, both residing in the region of the heart.

Chanting

An important form of meditation is the chanting of a *mantra*. Mantra means "that which delivers the mind." In other words, a mantra helps free the mind from worrying about temporary things such as money, shopping, health, and so on. It helps people to think clearly. In a state of peace, one becomes happy, free from yearning, fear, and lamentation.

A mantra is a short prayer or a string of sacred syllables. It may begin with the sacred syllable *Om*. The practice of chanting mantras quietly, or silently in the mind, is called *japa*. Mantras are also chanted loudly to music. This is called *kirtan*.

➤ *A sannyasi (see page 35) fingers prayer beads (japa-mala) during his meditation. He has taken a vow to chant almost seven thousand mantras each day, using the beads to help him count. There are usually 108 beads on each string.*

Mantras

Common mantras include:
- *"Om Namah Shivaya" ("I bow down and offer my respects to Lord Shiva")*

- *"Hare Krishna Hare Krishna, Krishna Krishna Hare Hare, Hare Rama Hare Rama, Rama Rama Hare Hare" ("Oh Krishna, Oh Rama, please engage me in your service")*

- *The Gayatri mantra (see page 33).*

Festivals

In Hinduism, hundreds of festivals occur every year, and they vary according to region and tradition. The four main purposes of festivals are: to celebrate special events in the life of a specific deity, to mark seasonal changes and events connected to nature, to celebrate special events in the life of a holy person, and to celebrate family relationships.

Festivals of the first type are often celebrated widely throughout India and other parts of the world. Some are also public holidays.

The other festivals are more likely to be celebrated in one region of India or by people from that area and are often connected with a specific tradition, which may follow a particular saint.

Festivals are observed by fasting and feasting, visiting temples and relatives, wearing new clothes, and decorating homes and temples. The festivals also include much music, dance, and drama, as well as special acts of worship. For example, on Janmashtami (Krishna's birthday) there is a beautiful midnight arati.

Twelve Important Festivals

Name of festival	Time of year	Relevant figures and significance
1. Makara Sankranti	January	**Surya**: harvest festival (called Pongal in southern India)
2. Sarasvati Puja	January/February	**Sarasvati** (birthday) and beginning of spring
3. Maha Shiva Ratri	February/March	**Shiva**
4. Holi	March	**Vishnu** (man-lion avatar) and spring festival
5. Rama Navami	March/April	**Rama** (birthday)
6. Hanuman Jayanti	April	**Hanuman** (birthday)
7. Guru Puja	July	**Sage Vyasa** and one's personal guru
8. Raksha Bandana	August	Brothers and sisters
9. Janmashtami	August/September	**Krishna** (birthday)
10. Ganesh Chaturthi	August/September	**Ganesh** (birthday)
11. Nava Ratri	Sept./October	**Shakti** (Parvati, Durga, and other goddesses)
12. Diwali	Oct./November	**Lakshmi** (also Rama): for some, the New Year

The Hindu Calendar

According to the Gregorian (or Western) calendar, Hindu festivals fall on different dates each year. This is because the Hindu months correspond to the actual cycles of the moon. The twelve Hindu months are shorter than months in the Western calendar, and so a leap month (extra month) is added once every three years. A Hindu month has thirty days, although one day is occasionally skipped. The month is divided into two halves —the light fortnight, as the moon waxes, and the dark fortnight, as it wanes. In everyday affairs, Hindus often use Western calendars, but religious observances are still worked out according to the lunar calendar.

New Year and Diwali

Hindus celebrate the New Year at different times. For many, it coincides with Diwali (the Festival of Lights). This autumn festival welcomes Lakshmi, the goddess of prosperity, into the home. It also commemorates the victorious return of Rama and Sita, as told in the *Ramayana*, and their entrance into their capital city, Ayodhya (*see page 19*).

▼ *Diwali celebrations in the UK. Diwali means "row of lamps." During the festival, Hindus decorate homes and temples inside and out with thousands of divas (lamps).*

Spring Festivals

One of the first festivals in the Hindu year is dedicated to the worship of Sarasvati, the goddess of learning and the arts. On this day, Hindus welcome spring by wearing yellow clothes, and children fly brightly colored kites. Shortly afterward comes the biggest festival for worshipers of Shiva. It is called Maha Shiva Ratri—the great night of Shiva. Strict worshipers fast for twenty-four hours and stay up all night to attend the puja (ritual worship) of the *linga*, a stone column representing Lord Shiva.

Holi

Perhaps the most famous spring festival is Holi. It recalls the story of the saint Prahlad and the half-man, half-lion incarnation of Vishnsu.

In this story, Prince Prahlad's tyrannical father was trying to kill his son. After many unsuccessful attempts, the king asked his sister, Holika, for help. Holika had been granted a boon by the fire-god Agni that gave her special protection from fire. To help her evil brother, she carried Prahlad into the middle of a raging bonfire. Vishnu, however, protected the boy and the wicked Holika burned to ashes.

Hindus celebrate this event and spring by building huge bonfires. On this day, everyone is allowed to be sassy, even to teachers and parents! Children and adults all have fun by playing tricks and throwing colored powder and water over each other.

In Our Own Words

"Yesterday it was Holi. We went to the temple wearing white clothes and threw colored water all over each other. We got completely covered in it! My friends played tricks, too, like hiding from each other. We did this to remember how Krishna loved playing tricks when he was young. Then we ate long noodles, boiled with sugar and ghee."

◄ Holi celebrations and fun in Pushkar, India. During Holi, Hindus hurl colored powders and water at each other. They believe that Krishna also played like this thousands of years ago. Krishna's birthday, called Janmashtami, falls in summer, not long after Raksha Bandana (see page 29).

Nava Ratri

The longest festival, Nava Ratri, occurs in late autumn. Nava Ratri means "nine nights," and over nine consecutive evenings, Hindu people meet to worship the goddess Shakti. The favorite activity for worship are exuberant stick dances, with all the women and girls dressed in bright saris.

Nava Ratri specifically honors Shakti, the wife of Shiva. She is often addressed as "Devi" (goddess) and as "Mataji" (respected mother). In Bengal, Devi is worshiped in the form of Durga, who rides on a lion and wields weapons in her ten hands.

▼ *A brother and sister in the United States celebrate the festival of Raksha Bandana. It is observed in August, mainly in the home. Females tie rakhis (protective bracelets) on the wrists of their brothers and other male relatives—even close family friends. The boys and men respond by giving gifts to their sisters.*

In Our Own Words

"We celebrate Raksha Bandana at home. I say a prayer asking Bhagwan (God) to protect Vijay, my brother. I then tie a rakhi bracelet, usually made of gold or silver thread, on Vijay's wrist. In return, he gives me a present and promises to look after me."

Pilgrimage

Visiting holy places is an integral part of the Hindu way of life. Hindus undertake pilgrimage for a number of reasons: to remember and worship the divine (God, a specific deity, or a particular saint), for purification to make spiritual progress, or to perform a religious rite or ritual, such as a ceremony for a deceased person.

▼ *Bathing ghats and a shrine dedicated to Shiva honor the banks of the River Ganges in Varanasi.*

Practices

When traveling, Hindus often accept voluntary hardships (austerity). These hardships can include fasting, celibacy, or travelling barefoot—also a sign of respect for sacred ground. They visit special shrines, marking the birthplace of a saint or other events associated with a story or legend. Pilgrims take darshan (sight) of the murti, receive holy food (prasad), and give in charity to the shrine, holy people, and the poor. They may hear stories connected with the site and often show respect by walking reverentially around the spot, usually in a clockwise direction.

Holy Places

Most Hindu holy sites are in India and connected with a particular deity. The most famous place, Varanasi, in the northeast of India, is devoted to Lord Shiva. It is also called Benares and Kashi. Here, pilgrims scatter the ashes of their loved ones in the sacred River Ganges, believing that this helps the soul toward final liberation.

About 1,000 miles (160 kilometers) south of Delhi, the holy towns of Mathura and Vrindavan are connected to Krishna who lived there as a child and youth. On the east coast, the town of Puri is famous for its annual "festival of the chariots," now celebrated throughout the world. In the north of the country, in the foothills of the Himalayas, there is a hilltop shrine at Vaishnoo Devi. It attracts many pilgrims and is dedicated to the three main female deities—Lakshmi, Sarasvati, and Shakti (in her fierce form as Goddess Kali).

Sacred Mountains and Rivers

The Himalayas are sacred to many Hindus. In these remote peaks, and in the surrounding foothills, yogis and ascetics perform penance, doing meditation and tolerating the chilling cold. Further south, in a region that gets scorching hot in summer, lies the famous hill called Govardhana. Pilgrims offer respect by walking around it while praying. The *Puranas* tell the story of how Krishna lifted the hill to protect the local people from torrential rain sent by the rain god, Indra.

Many rivers are considered sacred by Hindus. There are seven major holy rivers, of which the Ganges is most important, and bathing in them is thought to wash away one's sins (or bad karma). One of the biggest events is the Kumbha Mela (bathing fair) held regularly in different towns. The *Puranas* tell the story of how the gods and their enemies, the demons, came to a truce. By churning the ocean, they produced the nectar of immortality. The nectar fell at certain spots in India, where the Kumbha Melas now take place. Hindus believe that bathing in these places can grant moksha (liberation). In 2001, the Kumbha Mela in the town of Prayag attracted well over twenty million people!

▼ *Pilgrims bathe in the sacred River Ganges during Kumbha Mela.*

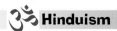

Rites of Passage

For Hindus, life is an ongoing journey—a long adventure. Hindus believe that even before birth, one (the soul) has existed somewhere else. After death, one departs either to take another body or to get liberation (*see page 14*). This world is like a restaurant or a railway station, with people constantly arriving, meeting each other, then leaving.

For many Hindus, four principal stages (ashramas) occur throughout this one life—student life, householder life, retired life, and renounced life (*see page 14*). There are also up to sixteen main ceremonies, which celebrate the completion of one period of life (or an entire ashrama) and moving on to the next. These rituals are called *samskaras*. They help

▼ *This boy is about to have his first haircut. The priest is ringing a small bell, as is customary during worship and rituals. The birth and name-giving ceremonies are the fourth and fifth samskaras. They are followed by sixth, the first outing; seventh, the first grains; eighth, the first haircut; ninth, piercing of the ears.*

purify the soul so that it can be free from selfish thoughts and actions. This helps the individual move toward moksha (liberation).

Birth Ceremonies

The first samskara takes place before conception. The couple prays that a good soul will enter the womb. They want the baby to grow up to be a healthy person and a good citizen. During pregnancy, two other samskaras take place for the healthy development of both mother and child.

At birth, the *jatakarma* ceremony welcomes the baby into a new chapter of life—a new family. The father places a small amount of ghee (clarified butter) and honey on the child's tongue and whispers the name of God in the child's ear. Shortly afterward, a name-giving ceremony is performed in which the infant is dressed in new clothes. At this time, it is customary for a priest to make a horoscope for the child and to predict the future.

Initiation Ceremony

The next major ceremony, usually considered the tenth or eleventh samskara, occurs between the ages of eight and twelve. The boy is given a sacred thread and sometimes a new, spiritual name. He is then considered "twice-born," a full member of his varna (*see page 37*), and can begin chanting the Gayatri mantra (*see box*). This samskara represents a spiritual birth, and traditionally the boy accepts a guru (teacher).

A subsequent samskara marking the actual beginning of education may also occur, but today the two ceremonies are often performed together. In previous times, boys would go to live with their teacher and attend the *gurukula* (the traditional "school of the guru"). There they learned the *Vedas* and tried to develop good qualities, such as honesty, cleanliness, and an attitude of service to others.

The sacred thread ceremony is usually performed only for boys who are members of the three higher varnas: Vaishya, Kshatriya, and Brahmin (*see page 14*). Some religious groups perform the same ritual for girls, but women don't usually wear the sacred thread.

> ➤ *A boy in India at his sacred thread ceremony. The thread is draped over the left shoulder and falls diagonally across the body. After the ceremony, the boy regularly chants the Gayatri mantra three times each day—at dawn, noon, and dusk. As he recites this mantra, he will have his sacred thread wrapped around the thumb of his right hand.*

The Gayatri Mantra

"*We concentrate our minds on the most radiant light of the Sun god, who sustains the earth, the heavens, and all that lies in between. May he guide our intellect.*"

—Rig Veda *3.62.10*

The Wedding Ceremony

The wedding, the fifteenth samskara, is perhaps the most important ceremony in a Hindu's life. It marks the entrance into the household ashrama, the second stage of life (*see page 14*). Traditionally, parents arranged marriages, ensuring that the bride and groom shared similar tastes, interests, and backgrounds. Young Hindus usually had some say in the choice of partners. Today, couples often make arrangements independently of their parents.

The actual ceremony that celebrates a wedding varies according to region and tradition. Often, several ceremonies lead up to the main event. On the day itself, various rituals symbolize union. The couple exchange flower garlands, the priest pours water over their joined hands, and their upper garments are knotted together by a female relative to symbolize the union.

A priest performs a havan (sacred fire-ceremony). The couple tosses grains, symbolizing prosperity, into the fire and then walks around the fire together, usually four times. They then take seven steps together. Each step is to bring fulfillment of their wishes: for good food, wealth, health, children, and so on. The ceremony is concluded with relatives and friends offering gifts and blessings, all followed by a grand feast.

Retirement and Renounced Life

Within the Hindu community, divorce is now quite widespread, especially outside India. Traditional Hinduism disapproves of it, considering marriage a firm vow and a lifelong

▼ *A marriage ceremony in South India. The bride is dressed in the traditional red and gold sari and the groom wears white silk. Most ceremonies are lavish affairs and conclude several days of ritual celebration.*

commitment. In past times, when children were grown up and settled, their parents were expected to enter the third ashrama, retired life, often spending time on pilgrimage. Today, many couples retire from work, but few formally enter the third ashrama.

Only a few men adopt the fourth ashrama, renounced life. This involves leaving home to become a sannyasi (wandering monk) in order to prepare for death and the inevitable separation it brings. The sannyasi has to give up the idea that he belongs to a certain family, race, country, or religion. He becomes "a citizen of the world," trying to develop his love for God and to see all living beings equally. He also has responsibility to teach and preach, especially to householders who easily forget that all material situations are temporary. The wife of a sannyasi remains at home to dedicate herself to spiritual practices.

Funeral Rites

After death, Hindus usually cremate the body. They believe that this helps the soul move on to its destination. Otherwise, many believe it may hang around as a ghost, attached to the objects of its former life.

The body is first washed and decorated with new clothes and flower garlands. The eldest son lights the funeral pyre and the priest chants prayers, wishing the soul a safe journey. Afterward, the ashes are scattered in a holy river such as the Ganges. This sixteenth samskara signifies the end of another chapter of life.

▼ *A body burns on a funeral pyre in Kathmandu, Nepal. The ashes will be scattered in the Baghmati River. After the funeral, relatives observe a period of mourning to help them come to terms with their grief and which, Hindus believe, allows the departed soul to move on. Regular rituals are performed on the anniversary of the death.*

4 Society, Culture, and Lifestyle

Hinduism is not just a religion but a whole way of life. Until recently, Hindu culture was not separate from Hindu religion. Music, dance, and drama all depicted religious stories, and even dress and daily cooking were connected to spiritual practices. Similarly, the Hindu social system was based on religious ideas. One of the earliest texts, the Rig Veda, refers to four social classes called varnas. This developed into a more sophisticated system called "Varnashrama dharma" (see page 14). Later texts describe the different dharmas (duties) for people, based upon how they belong to four varnas and four ashramas (stages of life).

◄ A traditional dance-drama in Bali, Indonesia, telling the famous story of Rama and Sita. Hindu culture is rich in such tales, depicting learned saints, chivalrous kings, beautiful princesses, and wicked demons. These tales often reflect the Hindu ideal of interdependence—the idea that we all have different, but equally valuable, roles in society. They also teach about human virtues such as honesty, wisdom, courage, conquering evil, and protecting the innocent.

➤ *This diagram, based on a passage in the* Rig Veda, *shows how each varna is related to a part of "the social body." The four varnas are: 1. priests and teachers 2. government, army, and police 3. business people, traders, and farmers 4. craftspeople, artists, and workers.*

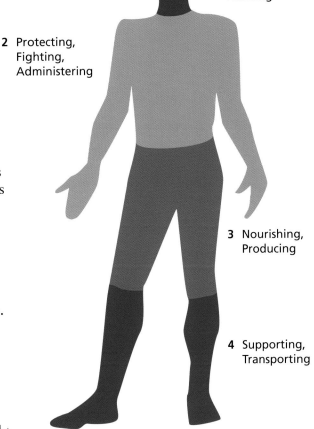

1 Vision, Thinking, Listening, Advising

2 Protecting, Fighting, Administering

3 Nourishing, Producing

4 Supporting, Transporting

The Four Varnas

According to the *Bhagavad Gita*, people belong to a particular varna according to their personal qualities and the job that suits them. The four varnas are like different parts of the social body. Each part of the human body is essential and works with others for the benefit of the whole body (*see diagram*). Similarly, the idea of the four varnas was to help society run smoothly. Many Hindus claim that, in this original system, people were allowed to move freely between varnas.

The Caste System

Over the centuries, the Hindu social system changed. Some brahmins, traditionally unattached to material things, became protective of their high positions. They taught that once born into a varna, a person cannot move from it. This protected brahmin families and their descendants from being demoted to lower classes. It doomed those born in lower varnas, no matter what their abilities, to stay in lowly occupations for successive generations.

Foreigners to India used the Portuguese word "casta" to describe this system, from which the English word "caste" originates. Besides the four varnas, thousands of sub-groups called *jati* also exist. A jati often describes the exact job a person does, rather like the origins of English surnames such as "Taylor" (tailor) and "Smith" (blacksmith). Even today, Hindus are often still expected to marry someone from the same varna and jati.

In Our Own Words

"My father, like my mother, was born in a brahmin family, but he is a businessman. He doesn't mind if I later get married to someone outside our community. He's religious but also very open-minded. I think that the caste system is a problem in Hinduism. Perhaps the original system was okay, but I feel that more recently it has become corrupt."

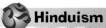

▲ *Mahatma Gandhi. Like him, many modern Hindus disagree with the hereditary caste system. Gandhi is also famous for teaching about ahimsa (nonviolence).*

Mahatma Gandhi

Mahatma Gandhi (1869–1947) was a holy man, politician, and probably the best-known Indian of the twentieth century. He helped to negotiate Indian independence from British colonial rule, but he was bitterly disappointed by the partition of his beloved country (*see page 10*). He was assassinated in 1947.

Gandhi drew much of his strength and conviction from the Hindu teachings, but he objected to the hereditary caste system. By that time, some Hindus had been called "untouchables," indicating that they were lower than even the fourth varna. They were given only the lowest jobs, such as cleaning the streets or working with leather. They were often banned from eating with others, entering temples, or drawing water from village wells. Gandhi renamed those called the "untouchables" "the children of God," to show his idea that everyone, having an eternal soul within, is equally important.

"Gautama's Disciple"

(from the Jabala Upanishad*)*

"A young boy approached Gautama Muni and begged to become his student. It was customary that only brahmins would be accepted for such spiritual training. Gautama therefore asked, 'Who is your father?' 'That I do not know,' the boy replied. 'So, please ask your mother.' The boy's mother admitted, 'My dear son, I have known many men. I do not know who is your father.' The boy returned to Gautama Muni and relayed the message, 'Sir, my mother also does not know who my father is.' Gautama Muni concluded, 'Yes, you are a brahmin. I accept you because you are thoroughly honest.'"

For practical purposes, Gandhi believed in the system of four varnas but not in the caste system, which was determined by birth and did not allow equal opportunity for all.

The Four Ashramas

The Sanskrit word ashrama has been taken into English as "ashram," meaning "hermitage," or "place of retreat." Its literal meaning in Sanskrit is "a place to develop spiritual understanding," indicating that all four ashramas are meant for spiritual growth.

The four traditional stages of life have never been followed by all Hindus, and today few Hindus strictly follow the rules of the ashramas. Nonetheless, the idea of a life of spiritual education—followed by material enjoyment and ultimate withdrawal from society—remains an important ideal.

Family Life

Although Hinduism places great value on ultimate detachment from worldly pleasure, it simultaneously stresses the importance of family stability. The building block of Hindu society is the extended family, consisting of three or four generations living together or near to each other. Great respect was traditionally given to family elders, who would offer guidance to younger members. The center of practically every Hindu home is the shrine, showing that one's relationship with God should be the main focus within the family.

Women in Hinduism

Traditionally, Hindu men and women took different roles. A woman's main role was as a housewife, while a man was solely responsible for earning the family's income. These roles have changed in modern society, and many Hindu women now pursue careers outside the home. Nonetheless, they often retain their traditional values, believing that by God's arrangement men and women can play complementary, and equally important, roles.

Often stories in the news tell about how women are mistreated in India. Some families try to secure wealth illegally by abusing the ancient system of dowry (a gift of money given to the bride by her family). These crimes are largely due to greed, poverty, and other social pressures, rather than religion. Hindu texts, such as the *Mahabharata*, explain that anyone who abuses women will lose all good karma, thus diminishing their health, wealth, and longevity.

Caring for Others

Hindu scripture teaches that a good government looks after five sections of society: women, children, animals, holy people, and the elderly. Any society can be judged by how well it protects these five types of citizens. For example, when Hindu people retire, their children usually look after them. Within the home, children are taught to respect visiting gurus and sannyasis, who help householders remember their spiritual goals. The whole purpose of the Varnashrama dharma system (*see page 14*) is for the strong to protect the weak and not to exploit them.

➤ *A Hindu family in the UK enjoys a picnic. Children's welfare has been the main focus of family life. A prominent Hindu ideal is giving shelter to dependents and not abusing their trust. For this reason, and through belief in reincarnation, Hindu texts do not sanction abortion and recommend that meat-eating be given up, or at least restricted.*

Sacred Food

Food is so important to Hindus that the tradition has been dubbed "the kitchen religion." Offering food to God is an essential item of temple puja (worship). Similarly, at home, some families eat only after the meal has been offered on the family shrine. It then becomes prasad, sacred food, which Hindus believe purifies the body, mind, and soul.

Believing the soul to be present in all species, many Hindus practice ahimsa (nonviolence) and are vegetarian. Meat is now becoming popular with those living in the West, but very few eat beef, out of reverence toward the cow and bull. In India, meat is often eaten only after ritual sacrifice to the goddess Kali (a fierce form of Shakti).

Hospitality

A popular Hindu proverb states, "the unexpected guest should be treated as well as God." Many stories show the importance of offering hospitality. A Hindu should welcome a guest with at least three items— a place to sit, pleasant words, and refreshments. Hindu scriptures state that even an enemy should be treated this way! It is especially important to receive holy people into the home, to offer them *seva* (selfless service), and to inquire from them about the importance of spiritual life.

Hospitality and humility are two of the most important values of Hinduism. These values are based on the core belief that everyone should be honored as a part of the divine.

▼ *Food is offered before the shrine in a temple in the UK as part of Diwali celebrations* (see page 27).

Hindu Arts

Hindu teachings are also expressed though the arts. Until recently, almost all Indian music, dance, and drama had religious themes. The performing arts are often a form of worship, and the first dances were staged in temples. On festival days, stories from the epics and *Puranas* are still enacted on stage.

The visual arts are represented in many temples. Posters of the many saints and deities hang on the walls, and traditional paintings depict religious stories. One of the

▲ *A performance of* Kathakali, *a blend of dance and drama from the south Indian state of Kerala. It is typified by colorful and elaborate face masks depicting characters from Hindu scriptures, such as the* Ramayana, *the* Mahabharata, *and the* Puranas. *This performance is in Kerala itself.*

most lasting achievements of Hindu culture, however, is its architecture. Temples in southern Indian are famous for their colossal gateways that are decorated with hundreds of statues of various gods and goddesses.

Village Life

Hinduism developed largely in a rural setting, in the Indian countryside. Gandhi believed that the key to India's wealth and happiness lay in its villages. He worked daily at a spinning wheel and opposed the mechanization of industry, preferring instead simple cottage industries. Hindu texts state that prosperity consists not of paper money but of natural resources, such as land and animals. Nature's gifts provide the necessities of life, such as food, clothes, and shelter, and luxuries such as gold, silver, and jewels. Wealth comes by God's grace, not through human endeavor alone. India, however, is now beset by poverty. Many Hindus believe that it was far more prosperous before British colonialization and industrialization.

The religious practices in rural India are often different from those of the towns and cities. The focus is often on local deities and those that protect the village. The temples are generally smaller than in the cities, and there are many small outdoor shrines. Hindu texts suggest that living in the countryside helps people more easily remember God.

To Hindus, the cow and bull are considered important. The cow provides milk, from which to make yogurt, cream, butter, and ghee (clarified butter, used in cooking as well as temple rituals). Dairy products are vital to those who follow a vegetarian diet. Because the cow provides milk, Hindus consider her to be "mother," and in this sense she is sacred. She also represents mother earth. Bulls are still used for ploughing, milling, and transporting. Despite widespread introduction of the tractor, for many poorer Indians the bull remains an important source of energy.

▼ *Girls carry their calves in a typical Indian village near Vrindavan, the sacred town connected to Lord Krishna. Krishna himself fondly looked after cows.*

5 Hinduism in Today's World

Today, an increasing number of Hindus live in sprawling cities, such as Mumbai, Kolkata, Chennai, and New Delhi. Many live overseas. With increased migration and the rise of global communications, Hinduism has moved from its ancient, rural, and Indian context to play a strong role in many of today's multicultural societies.

An Indian Religion?

Hindu people face many challenges as they adapt to the rapidly changing world. Even the idea of Hinduism as a single religion like other "world faiths" is relatively new. Some Hindus strongly identify their religion with India and promote forms of Hindu nationalism. They are often concerned about attempts to convert Hindus to other religions. Other thinkers emphasize that Hinduism—the Sanatan Dharma—extends beyond India. It is a spiritual path open to everyone.

Ancient or Modern?

Tensions abound between ancient practices and modern values. For many Hindus, castes remain a fundamental part of their social and religious life. It is a much-debated issue. Many Hindus feel castes should be thrown out altogether. Others claim that the old system of four varnas is a useful way of organizing society, provided it is based on equal opportunity. There is also debate about the role of women. Again, some prefer modern ideas of equality. Others say that there is still value in traditional ideas, such as recognizing the differences between the sexes and their interdependent roles.

▼ A modern Hindu temple in the city of Durban, South Africa. Here, as elsewhere, Hinduism is often challenged by the tensions between old and new and between living in India and outside, in a different culture. Many Hindus believe that their ideas of spiritual equality and practices, such as yoga, are just as relevant in modern South Africa as they were in ancient India.

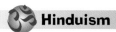

Toward a Healthy Planet

Many Hindus are actively interested in showing how their philosophy and values can be applied in modern life. Historically, India has already made significant contributions to world culture, the arts, and science. Historians say that the numeral zero originally came from India, and Hindu writings deal with astronomy, chemistry, and psychology. Indian medicine is known as Ayur Veda. It stresses the importance of a healthy diet, a balanced lifestyle, and herbal remedies. Today, it is becoming increasingly popular in the West, as an alternative or complementary medicine.

Hindu people are also contributing toward preserving the environment. Hindu scriptures mention the benefits of a natural life, planting trees, protecting wildlife, and avoiding pollution. The Hindu philosophy warns against greed and recommends sustainability and long-term vision as important moral principles.

▼ *School children in Northern India take part in an environmental project aiming to preserve local forests and their wildlife. Similar projects seek to protect the rivers, sacred to Hindus, that are threatened by deforestation and pollution. Many Hindus believe that traditional values, such as nonviolence and sustainability, can help address these global problems.*

The World as One Family

Dealing with the consequences of environmental exploitation is one of the greatest challenges of the twenty-first century. Another is the growing dominance of human abuse and conflict in the world—terrorism, indiscriminate war, economic exploitation, and many other forms of oppression.

Hindu teachings suggest that these conflicts are due to a wrong perception of identity—a mistaken idea of who we are. Hinduism teaches that many people wrongly believe that the body is the self and that happiness comes solely though physical gratification. Also, failing to see the real person within, they tend to judge others by their bodies, seeing them as black or white, male or female, young or old. They are prone to use these bodily labels to determine who is a friend or who is an enemy. Some people may even judge others as good or bad simply by the religion they follow.

In contrast, the Hindu motto "*Vasudaiva Kutumbakam*" means "the world is one family." This family includes not only humans but all other forms of life. In all living beings, the soul (atman) is present, and despite the different ways we think of God, he (and she) is the same for all of us. This is the core message of Hinduism, the Sanatan Dharma.

A Prayer for the Twenty-first Century

"May there be good fortune throughout the universe, and may all envious persons be pacified. May all creatures become calm by practicing bhakti-yoga, for by accepting devotional service they will think of each other's welfare. Therefore, let us all engage in the service of the one Supreme Lord!"

▼ *Hindu priests and an Anglican vicar at an interfaith event in England. Many Hindus believe that all great religious teachers have taught similar truths, with some differences in details according to the prevalent culture and the people they were teaching. Most, if not all, religious teachers have stressed the unity of humanity and of all of God's creation.*

Glossary

ahimsa the Sanskrit word for "nonviolence"

arati the most popular Hindu ceremony in which a lamp and other auspicious articles are offered to the sacred image

Aryan according to Hindu texts, the "noble people." Scholars say that the Aryans are a specific race who brought core Hindu teachings to India

ascetic a person who deliberately accepts physical hardship, usually to progress in spiritual life

ashrama a place where spiritual life is cultivated; one of the four stages in life

atman ("self") can mean body, mind, or soul, but ultimately refers to the "real self," the soul.

avatar a "descent" of God or a great soul from the spiritual (eternal) world. Often translated as "incarnation"

Bhagwan (Bhagavan) the most commonly used Indian term for God

bhajan ("worship") specifically refers to a hymn or religious song

bhakti ("devotion") Bhakti-yoga means the path of devotional service

Brahma the creator, one of the trimurti, the three main deities

Brahman the "Supreme" or "spirit," which is eternal and which pervades and supports everything

Brahmin a member of the highest varna; a priest, teacher, or intellectual

caste system a social system based on four varnas and other sub-groups; specifically, the system determined by birth rather than qualification

darshan ("seeing") taking audience of the deity or a holy person

guru a spiritual teacher. A regular teacher may also be called "guru"

hatha yoga a system of yoga based on physical exercises

havan the ancient sacred fire ceremony, still practiced on special occasions

japa the practice of repeating mantras quietly or silently, often while counting the mantras on prayer beads

jati occupational sub-groups that form part of the caste system

karma "action," also "the results of actions"

kirtan "glorification" usually refers to the musical chanting of mantras

Lakshmi the goddess of luck and prosperity, wife of Vishnu

linga a form of Shiva as a rounded, cylindrical stone

mantra a prayer or a string of sacred symbols

meditation the action of concentrating the mind and fixing it on a single point

moksha liberation from the perpetual cycle of repeated birth and death

murti a sacred image or statue, worshiped in the temple or home. It represents God or a particular god or goddess

penance accepting physical difficulties in order to make up for something one has done wrong

pradakshina circumambulation (walking reverentially around); an important feature of worship

prasada ("mercy") usually refers to sanctified, blessed food, offered to God

pravachan a talk or lecture on spiritual subjects

puja ritualistic worship, most often of the murti

Rama an important deity, usually considered to be the seventh avatar, or incarnation, of Vishnu

reincarnation the process of the soul entering one body after another in a series of births, lives, and deaths

sampradaya an unbroken line of gurus and disciples that transmits religious knowledge through the ages

samsara the perpetual cycle of repeated birth and death

samskara ("impression on the mind") refers to the various rites of passage

Sanatan Dharma ("the eternal religion") the eternal function of the soul, which is to serve God; another name for Hinduism

sannyasi a member of the fourth ashrama (stage of life)

Sanskrit an ancient Indian language, still used in worship today

Sarasvati the goddess in charge of learning and the arts; the wife of Brahma

seva the Sanskrit word for "service," a important Hindu principle and value

Shakti a female deity, especially the wife of Shiva (Parvati or Durga)

Shiva the destroyer; one of the trimurti, the three principal deities

Sikhism the religion founded in the sixteenth century by Guru Nanak

soul in Hinduism, the real, unchanging self, different from mind and body

trimurti the three main deities: Brahma (the creator), Vishnu (the sustainer), and Shiva (the destroyer)

untouchables people considered to fall outside the four varnas

varna a class or social group, originally based on peoples' qualities and inclination for a particular type of work. Over time, these classes became hereditary (determined by birth)

Varnashrama Dharma the ancient Hindu social system with different duties allocated to four varnas (classes) and four ashramas (stages in life).

Veda "knowledge;" the four *Vedas* are important Hindu holy books

Vishnu "the sustainer;" one of the trimurti, famous for his many avatars, or incarnations, such as Rama and Krishna

yoga "union," specifically with God, or any practice aimed at such realization

yogi (feminine: yogini) any person who seriously performs yoga

yuga ('age') four main ages that rotate like the seasons

Time Line

c. 3000 B.C.E.	According to Hindu tradition, Krishna appears on earth and speaks the *Bhagavad Gita* (Song of God). The beginning of Kali yuga (age of quarrel)
c. 2500 B.C.E.	Civilizations of Indus and Sarasvati valleys at height of their powers
c. 1500 B.C.E.	Aryans invade India, bringing the beginnings of Hinduism
c. 1500–500 B.C.E.	*Vedas* composed in the ancient language of Sanskrit
c. 500 B.C.E.–500 C.E.	Buddhism spreads throughout India. The *Puranas* and the epics (including the *Ramayana*) written
326–184 B.C.E.	Mauryan Empire unites much of India
320–550 C.E.	Reign of the Gupta dynasty, golden age for Hindu arts
500–1000 C.E.	Saints in South India compose many devotional poems
800	Shankara re-establishes importance of the Hindu holy books and Buddhism declines in India
c. 1050	Ramanuja teaches that God is personal, living beyond this world
1200–1500	Muslims become powerful in the north, but Hindu kingdoms flourish in the south of India
1469	Birth of Guru Nanak, founder of Sikh religion
1526	Mogul Empire founded in India. Many Bhakti saints live around this period
1600s and 1700s	Many Europeans arrive in India, mainly to trade
1757	India comes under British domination, becoming part of the Empire in 1858
1830 onward	Many Hindus migrate to Fiji, Malaysia, Mauritius, the Caribbean, East Africa and South Africa
1869	Birth of Mahatma Gandhi, leader in the struggle for Indian independence
1897	Ramakrishna Mission established in Calcutta by Swami Vivekananda
1947	India gains independence but loses territory to the newly-created Pakistan
1950s–1970s	Many Hindus migrate to North America (from India), to the UK (from East Africa and India) and to other countries, such as Holland and Australia
1960s	Indian thought and practices (e.g. yoga) become popular in the West with groups such as Transcendental Meditation and the Hare Krishna Movement
1990 onward	Hindus become socially, academically, and economically well-established in the West, building many large temples

Books

Das, Rasamandala. *Places of Worship: Hindu Temples.* Heinemann Educatonal Books—Library Division, 1999.

Ganeri, Anita. *Hindu Festivals through the Year.* Franklin Watts, 2003.

Lovelace, Ann and Joy White. *Beliefs Values and Traditions: Hinduism.* Heinemann, 1997.

Marchant, Kerena. *Krishna and Hinduism.* Smart Apple Media, 2003.

Robinson, James B. *Hinduism.* Chelsea House Publishers, 2004.

Web Sites

sanskrit.bhaarat.com/Dale/

www.advaita-vedanta.org/avhp/sankara-life.html

www.angelfire.com/ms/krishnapage/index.html

www.avatara.org/

www.koausa.org/Gods/index.html

www.palaceofgold.com/

www.seattleartmuseum.org/exhibit/interactives/ intimateWorlds/enter.asp

Index